12 PILLARS
of
DEPRESSION

Morgan Mortensen

12 PILLARS
of
DEPRESSION

Morgan Mortensen

International Psychoanalytic Books (IPBooks)

New York ♦ www.IPBooks.net

Copyright 2021 by Morgan Mortensen

International Psychoanalytic Books (IPBooks)
Queens, NY
Online at: IPBooks.net

All rights reserved. This book may not be reproduced, transmitted, or stored, in whole or in part by any means, including graphic, electronic, or mechanical without the express permission of the author and/or publisher, except in the case of brief quotations embodied in critical articles and reviews.

ISBN: 978-1-949093-85-8

To David, Brooke, Kara, and Dana

CONTENTS

Introduction	1
Preface	7
Pillar Month One	11
Pillar Month Two	19
Pillar Month Three	25
Pillar Month Four	31
Pillar Month Five	37
Pillar Month Six	43
Pillar Month Seven	49
Pillar Month Eight	55
Pillar Month Nine	61
Pillar Month Ten	67
Pillar Month Eleven	73
Pillar Month Twelve	79

INTRODUCTION

The grips of depression are impossible to explain unless you have experienced the dark corridors that inhabit your mind when in the state of depression. I have been told that I feel sorry for myself, should get over it, it is just a matter of feeling gratitude and the advice goes on and on. However, as any medical professional who treats depression knows the brain neurons and pathways are compromised, also the hormones that contribute to a feeling of well being are in short supply or entirely absent as well. Therefore DEPRESSION IS NOT JUST A MATTER OF ATTITUDE but of shortfalls in brain functioning. Once I understood that my depression was not just due to a faulty "me" (which can make a person even more depressed), but due to inadequate brain functions and the surrounding hormonal environment, then I had hope that these functions could be improved which made me feel less "defective". Western medicine concentrates on interventions focused on pharmaceuticals with talk therapy that can result in the patient feeling no improvement or experiencing the side effects from the medication. The pill is like a band aid on a cut but true brain function (neuronal and hormonal) needs to be generated from the brain itself. I experienced no improvement and only side effects after thirty different prescriptions and was labeled "treatment resistant". When I started researching Western medicine and holistic practices it literally opened up a whole new world to me of healing and improvement. I started my quest with a foundation of knowing that if I improved my neuronal pathways and how the brain is capable of repairing itself, for example, I would lessen my depression. If you change your thinking PATTERNS then new neuronal PATHWAYS are created due to the different energy levels created. The elimination of RUMINATION (incessant negative mind chatter) showed that my improvement would not just be a matter of my attitude and my faulty character but due to changes in the brain pathways that I could initiate. The pathways are regenerated when we have higher levels of energy through our behavior thus affecting our emotions and elevating our mood. These brain changes then softly but surely started to lessen the dark and heavy feelings of depression that I had experienced for a decade. I call these THE TWELVE PILLARS TO OVERCOME DEPRESSION. Our behavior manifests itself in permanent mental changes which requires THREE WEEKS to change so I embraced one PILLAR (behavior/thought) every day for a month. Keep a log for that month with a check mark for that monthly PILLAR by checking it off for that day that targeting that behavior/thought. Consistency is everything. This practice started improving my neuronal pathways and the good feeling hormones leading to a lessening of the depression. Then move on to the next PILLAR for the next month. The PILLARS are simple, clear and consistent but they must be repeated daily every day to take effect. When you start reaping the feeling of increased neuronal brain activity and the good feeling hormones it feels as if a miracle has occurred. Bless you on your journey.

PILLAR MONTH ONE:

Every day for one month I will tell myself that I am here for a reason. I may not know what that reason is but I would not be here unless I was supposed to be period. There is no other person exactly like me. (Followed by a detailed explanation and everyday situations).

PILLAR MONTH TWO:

I will live each day with the knowledge that behavior contributes to making the world a better place. This may be as simple as holding the door open for a senior citizen. (Followed by a detailed explanation and everyday situations).

PILLAR MONTH THREE:

I will try to get at least one person to smile a day with my own smile or a kind word. It does not matter if some people do not acknowledge it you do not know what their script is. (Followed by a detailed explanation and everyday situations).

PILLAR MONTH FOUR:

Talk to yourself as you would a friend including not being more judgmental on yourself than you would be to that friend. (Followed by a detailed explanation and everyday situations).

PILLAR MONTH FIVE:

Every time you start to compare stop. The grass always seems greener on the other side of the fence but you only have a very small snapshot of the other persons life. Comparing is an invitation to feeling insecure and more worthless. (Followed by a detailed explanation and everyday situations).

PILLAR MONTH SIX:

I will remind myself that fortune and fame is not what makes a person content and you cannot take fame and fortune with you when you pass. What is eternal is how you treat others. Do not engage in arguments and realize that if the other person was truly content that they would not be behaving this way. (Followed by a detailed explanation and everyday examples).

PILLAR MONTH SEVEN:

Stay in the PRESENT moment. Do not think about the past or the future. Think about TODAY only. (Followed by a detailed explanation and everyday examples).

PILLAR MONTH EIGHT:

Every time you have a negative thought that keeps going over and over recognize it and tell yourself «stop» and think of someone or something that makes you smile (a pet). (Followed by a detailed explanation and everyday examples).

PILLAR MONTH NINE:

Remind yourself that you have control over very little...not how other people react, if someone got the promotion and not you. We are too hard on ourselves over most events that are truly out of our control. (Followed by a detailed explanation and everyday examples).

PILLAR MONTH TEN:

Remind yourself that the love that you seek is within you and your heart. Do or say an act that conveys love to one person a day. It can be a word of appreciation to a customer service representative for their assistance. (Followed by a detailed explanation and everyday examples).

PILLAR MONTH ELEVEN:

Every interaction that I have with others is a teaching experience, especially the nasty ones. Ask yourself what the lesson that can be learned from this? (Followed by a detailed explanation and everyday examples).

PILLAR MONTH TWELVE:

I will give myself a daily compliment (as if to a friend) a word or deed that I did today which made the day a little brighter. (Followed by a detailed explanation and everyday examples).

A DAILY CHECKLIST AND LOG THAT IS BEAUTIFUL TO LOOK AT AND EASY TO CHECK OFF THESE ACTIVITIES.

PREFACE

The concept of "depression" is difficult to define. Depression is an illness in which the persistent emotion is sadness and the inability to complete daily activities or do activities that once were enjoyable. Brief episodes, depressed thoughts and negative feelings rise and fall, often for no apparent cause or reason with some depressive episodes. Severe forms of chronic depression, in contrast, can linger for weeks, months or years without end. Despair and desperation register in degraded moods of dejection, inadequacy, suppression, hopelessness, resignation, loss of energy, change in appetite, sleeping too much or too little or too much, lack of concentration. Chronic losses in vigor and vitality may also reduce or degrade the quality and intensity of motives, goals, and plans. Depression has a huge negative impact on the global economy with the reduced hours of work, impaired productivity, early retirement, and job insecurity. Depression globally is the largest contributor to job losses and disability that are non-fatal health loss. Depression is more common among women than men. Depression can affect every economic and educational level. Globally nearly five percent of the world's population has depression. Depression is a leading cause of disability across the workforce globally. Depressed people take more sick days and more likely to be unemployed.

The purpose of this handbook is to study the EXPERIENCE of depression and your role in changing darkness into lightness. Depression is treatable with the knowledge of how our thoughts and emotions increase the darkness or contribute to lightness and well-being. Descent into dark and somber outlooks are the warning signs of depression. Complex events do not always make good sense. One may fall into a bleak state of despair without knowing how or why to deal with such dark unexplained thoughts and feelings.

It is necessary, therefore, to make provision for practical mechanisms of relief and restoration. Just as dark covers up light, obscuring the clarity of body, mind, and spirit, so also can restored light lead the path to a whole brighter day. It takes consistency, courage, and a hopeful spirit to transform a dark outlook into a lighter mood. Gradual return to an elevated state of wellbeing and light can be obtained by adhering to the twelve pillars with their basic themes, in order to progress in matters of restored health and well-being. Depression is an illness need not be viewed as an obstacle to an improve state of mind and better health.

Our brains are capable of regeneration of neurons (neuroplasticity) and the production of the good feeling hormones (oxytocin, serotonin). The daily practice of implementing the twelve pillars (one pillar per month), requires three weeks of the targeted mindful activity to instill a strong healthy mindset. These TWELVE PILLARS consist of behavioral patterns that can change the way our brain neurons fire resulting in more positive automatic patterns. CONSISTENCY IS EVERYTHING. The TWELVE PILLARS are simple and clear, but they must be repeated as a daily activity to be effective. Embrace one pillar for every day of that month. At the end of each day make a check for that pillar. This practice is designed to improve brain function by generating new pathways from the behaviors implemented. The positive emotions that we evoke can also soothe distress and broaden our thinking patterns, resulting in the development of a more expansive outlook and view of our experiences thus uplifting our mood. The feeling of connectedness raises our energy level as we feel a part of humanity. The increased neuron activity along with the production of the good hormones that accompany this growth contribute to a feeling of being lighter so it will feel as is a small miracle is taking place.

NOTES

PILLAR MONTH ONE

Every day for one month I will tell myself that I am here for a reason. I may not know what that reason is but I would not be here unless I was supposed to be period. There is no other person exactly me. I would not be able to search for a compelling justification unless I possessed the need or desire to discover what my own life has to offeer other members of the human community. There is great comfort in knowing that I have the opportunity to make the world a better place. No other person can duplicate what I alone can contribute.

If you ever thought about it long and hard it is a miracle that any of us are here...what are the chances anyway. Of all the people that have ever lived, less than ten percent are alive today. The odds are incalculable. Some of the time the procreation that produced us is planned and sometimes it is a sheer accident. Once we are born some lives are saved by extraordinary means and some lives are lost. To think about life in this way means that you are still here for a reason and that reason is important. You may not know what that reason is right now but every person that is born is a source of light and love no matter how rich or poor they are, tall or short they are, these are qualities that we carry around with us as human beings. There are intrinsic factors, defining attributes, that we carry around with us regardless of our health and well-being. We need to remind ourselves that we are unique and distinctive human beings. Each of us has acquired a wide variety of abilities and skills that no one else can duplicate. Each active living being is a source of light and darkness.

Both positive and negative energy serve useful purposes. Positivity adds what negativity subtracts. Optimal conditions do not require the (total) presence of one emotion over the (complete) absence of another emotion. Being patient with yourself with depression matters equally as impatience with the perpetuation of depression.

The worst thoughts of criticism and judging ourselves comes from our own thoughts and negative viewpoints about ourselves. Negative self-talk may have to do with negative past experiences and beliefs, but it can also be a bad habit that built up a repertoire of negative self-talk and perceptions. We are not born with this negative self-talk so it was learned and therefore can be unlearned. Train yourself to focus and appreciate who you are. Remind yourself that you are unique and distinctive. Our emotional state and self-esteem end up in the lower vibrations and the hormones produced are the stress hormones when you think anything that makes you feel that you are not worthy period. No one else can take your place and you cannot take the place of anyone else either. What we need to remind ourselves is what is most important is that INSIDE IS WHO WE TRULY ARE AND THAT IS OUR BEAUTY. NO ONE CAN TAKE YOUR PLACE OR REPLACE YOU PERIOD.

The mystery of life does not reveal all of its secrets nor what makes life possible, necessary, or fragile. Our existence is not what we should try and figure out and strive to unravel. Instead, we need to remind ourselves that we are unique and distinctive. There is no exact duplicate or replica of you.

Internal discomfort occurs with emotions stemming from negative emotions such as fixing others, people pleasing, co-dependency, deprioritizing your own needs, fear of abandonment, tolerance of abuse from others, external validation needed, need to prove yourself, difficulty setting boundaries to name a few. These heavy emotions are evident when I was in a depression which only served to keep things heavy as if there was lead in my brain. This is an example of where a light thought turns in a dark thought. Chronically depressed do not value themselves. Profound feelings of inadequacy and inferiority only serve to depress light and magnify dark reflections. It is no wonder that depressed persons find it hard to laugh or to cry. Depressed people get trapped in a lack of creative energy that is a vicious cycle.

Think of one happy memory in your life, embrace it and realize that is the essence of your soul before bad things started to outweigh the good things in your mind and start to weigh you down with the depression. Embrace the happy thought and realize that it shapes the essence of who you are and what you have become. Realize that negative thoughts tend to attract more negative and dark thoughts therefore it is important to monitor and reframe them with a positive alternative as a means to reset the balance and restore some measure of harmony. I always thought that life made no sense. Life does not make sense a lot of the time so why do I keep trying to make it have sense...this does not help and keeps things heavy. This is an example of a light thought versus a heavy thought. Each time you think a light/positive thought versus a heavy/negative thought the patterns of thinking affect the neurons and hormones in your brain. When you have feelings of UNIQUENESS, this positive emotion will generate neuroplasticity, which is the ability of the brain to rewire itself with new pathways. The brain lays down new neural pathways in response to the higher and lighter vibrational levels. The combination of new cells and openness to learning is what allows the magic to happen.

No way of life is friction free—life does not unfold in a straight line. There is no master plan to guide our path from darkness to light. Blessings mingle with burdens. Two steps forward, one step backwards or the other way around. Change is a constant. What comes up must come down. Stop Reframe. Go slow. Try something different to get out of a rut. This too shall pass. Never lose heart. A hopeful, spirit should not be dismissed as having trivial value. A hopeful outlook gains traction over time. What makes the greatest magnitude of difference is the capacity and willingness to see there is light despite all the darkness.

I started to discover my reason for existence in a gradual manner. It started with a greater appreciation of the unique features of who I am and my viewpoint and daily existence. People who suffer from depression are literally "wired" for feeling sad and hopeless, but the laws of neuroplasticity tells us that this wiring can be enhanced with a change in our thinking. Neuroplasticity is present throughout your entire lifespan. With the lighter mindset the brain can heal and grow. Contrast this with the depressed person, who does not value themselves with feeling worthlessness. Profound feelings of inadequacy and inferiority only serve to depress light and magnify dark thoughts and reflections. Your thinking patterns are in the stress mode therefore low vibration pathways are working and the stress hormones are being produced. No wonder depressed people do not laugh. The view point that you should keep in mind when depressed is to realize is that no one thinks like you, laughs like you, writes like you, has the same hobbies as you, has the same likes and dislikes as you. If you were not here every one of those unique qualities would be missed and never duplicated again by anyone period. Just as no two snowflakes are ever alike. THERFORE YOU ARE NOT REPLACEABLE. These unique qualities that are yours and yours alone make you special and utterly one of a kind as well as unique period. Your own unique qualities can be that you are funny, pretty, odd, cute, bizarre, unusual, attractive, not so attractive, mainstream, not mainstream. UNIQUENESS WINS!

WRITE DOWN EVERY DAY SOME CHARACTERISTICS THAT YOU HAVE. YOU OWN THESE QUALITIES THESE ARE YOURS AND PRICELESS. REMIND YOURSELF DAILYPTHAT THESE LOVABLE AND UNIQUE TO YOU!

JANUARY

1.
2.
3.
4.
5.
6.
7.
8.
9.
10.
11.
12.
13.
14.
15.
16.
17.
18.
19.
20.
21.
22.
23.
24.
25.
26.
27.
28.
29.
30.
31.

NOTES

PILLAR MONTH TWO

I WILL LIVE EACH DAY WITH THE KNOWLEDGE THAT THE BEHAVIOR OF EACH PERSON CONTRIBUTES TO MAKING THE WORLD A BETTER PLACE. THIS BEHAVIOR MAY BE AS SIMPLE AS HOLDING THE DOOR OPEN FOR A SENIOR CITIZEN.

The internet and technology has the planet wired together and communicating as it never has before... or is it communication at all? Sure, it is instant feedback. Yes, it is across every country and continent on the planet, yet as human beings we are feeling more isolated and alone than ever before because of the decrease in human face to face interactions. Yes, we do have Zoom, but with the pandemic isolation parameters in place, mandating no social gatherings. Also with most of our work day behind our computer, without hearing the voice of the other person, which can reveal much information about them, we lose much of the complete picture that gives us an idea about the other person. Instead we sit behind our computers and communicate through our keyboards and screens while becoming more and more isolated. The increased isolation that we are seeing all across all cultures all over the world increases depression because people feel all alone. Human beings are social, and interaction is psychologically important for our sense of connectedness. The pandemic has escalated isolation with escalating depression and anxiety. This being said the depressed individual already feels terribly alone and isolated. Therapy activities can involve contact and reintegration with others to increase feelings of positive energy which helps the brain to stop thinking in the same negative neural pathways. When we are able to interact with others face to face the feelings of inclusiveness create the good feeling hormones that lessen the dark feelings of depression.

The depressed person feels very isolated so anything that increases feelings of being connected is a step towards overcoming depression. Research shows that learning and practicing loving acts of kindness can rewire your brain to be more in the present moment and boost your mood with enhanced neuron activity along with the production of good feeling hormones. A kind act or word given and the resulting smile that is received back can change the way a depressed person feels. Try opening the door for a senior citizen, let someone in ahead of you in the traffic line, wave hi to someone that you are walking past on the street. Let someone with groceries go ahead of you. Perform the act of kindness without any expectation of anything in return because sometimes this will happen…it does not matter…you are striving to make the world a better place and the positive feedback will cause the good hormones to be released thus decreasing the feelings of depression.

If you are able to tell someone thank you or give them a little token of appreciation for no reason it will give you more a sense of happiness than the receiver. Researchers have shown that acts of kindness elevates the mood of people when performed six times each week for a month. Loving kindness encourages practicing warm and tender thoughts towards others which produces greater positive emotions and has a lasting improved mood for the person practicing the kind act or word. This mood elevation will enhance neuroplasticity as the brain rewires itself resulting in the lessening of depression. Intentionally set a goal to practice ONE DAILY ACT OF LOVING KINDNESS. Express a kind word to a coworker. Make an effort to extend kind words to a neighbor. Pay a compliment to the drive-up worker. The act of helping others actually activates the part of the brain that makes you feel pleasure from the neuron activation and the production of good hormones such as oxytocin. The kinder that you act towards others the better you will feel. The quote from the Dalai Lama should be your motto "Be kind whenever possible. It is always possible".

WRITE DOWN EVERY DAY A KIND WORD OR DEED SAID TO ANOTHER THROUGHOUT THE DAY.

FEBRUARY

1.
2.
3.
4.
5.
6.
7.
8.
9.
10.
11.
12.
13.
14.
15.
16.
17.
18.
19.
20.
21.
22.
23.
24.
25.
26.
27.
28.
29.

NOTES

PILLAR MONTH THREE

I WILL TRY TO GET AT LEAST ONE PERSON TO SMILE A DAY WITH MY OWN SMILE OR KIND WORD (THE FOCUS IS ON VERBAL WHILE PILLAR TWO FOCUSED ON BEHAVIORAL). IT DOES NOT MATTER IF SOME PEOPLE DO NOT ACKNOWLEDGE YOU AS YOU NEED TO REMIND YOURSELF THAT YOU DO NOT KNOW WHAT THEIR INTERNAL SCRIPT IS.

I have tried smiling to people as I walk by and say hi with no expectation of a smile or a hi back in return but so often I receive back a surprised look and a smile with a hi. The depressed person is often feeling isolated, alone and misunderstood so to step outside that boundary and create a connection ever so small elevates the mood because of the feeling of connection. Picture children who do not have their guard up and when they are smiling…the hormones that accompany those elevated moods are flowing, they feel open and free to experience their surroundings.

The depressed person feels the opposite of that… isolated, alone, the stress hormones are prevalent. We see the ramifications of this severe isolation with the pandemic of COVID-19 throughout the world causing escalating depression and suicide rates. When people have more a sense of community and connection their despondence is not as severe with the ability to reach out and feel some form of connection thus the depression and stress levels decrease.

Also, if you really turn the focus on another person and their smile it naturally removes the focus of attention from yourself to them. When you receive that smile back it will give you a warm feeling which produces the good hormones and the brain activity is more optimal than when the focus of the thinking is on yourself while in the depressed state. A physician I had for depression asked me to think of a clown in a circus and the perpetual smile on their face. He told me to try practice putting that smile on on myself…it will have a positive domino affect.

This activity of obtaining smiles is also important for another reason…it makes you realize that everyone has their own story…so you need to expect no smiles back from some people. If you remind yourself not to take it personally it helps with the depression because you realize it is not just you with problems but that they have their own worries and troubles also. I am the type of person that attracts strangers who come up to me and start to tell me their troubles (make sure you are in a safe situation), and I always lend an ear.

Why do I bother? Because this is an act of kindness, such as a smile is an act of kindness. Kindness cultivates compassion and it generates a feeling that you made someone else feel better, thus you will notice you will feel better as well, even if you are suffering from some level of depression I assure you will feel lighter. In our contemporary society people are buried in their cell phones even while sitting at the table in a restaurant. When smiles are exchanged you know the mood has to be an elevated one while producing the good hormones and increased brain activity one step at a time. The exchange of smiles done daily will make a difference in elevating your mood.

NOTES

MARCH

1.
2.
3.
4.
5.
6.
7.
8.
9.
10.
11.
12.
13.
14.
15.
16.
17.
18.
19.
20.
21.
22.
23.
24.
25.
26.
27.
28.
29.
30.
31.

NOTES

PILLAR MONTH FOUR

TALK TO YOURSELF AS YOU WOULD A FRIEND INCLUDING NOT BEING MORE JUDGEMENTAL ON YOURSELF THAN YOU WOULD BE TO THAT FRIEND.

The depressed person is usually their own worst enemy and more critical on themselves than they would ever ever be on anyone else they care about such as a friend. This is a big part of the problem of depression as it generates low self esteem and self loathing which all contribute to the decrease of the good hormones in the brain and decreased brain function. The depressed person operates in this state of low mood physiologically and psychologically one affecting the other and it becomes a vicious circle. The bad self talk lowers the mood and the mood stays depressed creating a vicious bad habit of not to talk to kindly to yourself or not being able to think of your yourself in a positive way. The negativity pattern is a certain way of thinking following a pathway in the brain. Positive emotions create a new brain pathways and that is how positive talk can literally help with changed thought patterns when done consistently. This is what researchers mean when they talk about neuroplasticity. Therefore it is crucial that you play "LETS PRETEND" so that is how you are going to talk and treat yourself, as if you are your friend, maintaining the kind dialogue in regard to yourself.

Throughout the day remind yourself of something that your friend would say to while you are performing your work tasks, chores around your home, getting ready in the morning, choosing what to think, choosing what not to think, especially the self talk that goes on inside your head. The more compassion and kindness that you can give to yourself the more your brain releases the good hormones and activates more brain activity. The beauty of being kind to yourself, which is hard for depressed people to do, is that researchers found it lifts the person's mood for these reasons. For example, say to yourself when you make a mistake instead of "What a stupid thing that only I would do" reframe to what a friend or kind relative would say "Yes that was a mistake but I learned from it so I now know more than before this happened". When you look in the mirror and you want to focus on a physical attribute that you really intensely dislike, instead reframe what you focus on, then choose a positive or unique quality that you have. Talk to yourself about this quality as your friend would talk to you about it and in your friends words. This is reframing, you are looking at the cup half full and with kindness as your kind friend looks at you, instead of half empty and harshly as you usually look at yourself.

Some examples of talking kindly to yourself as you would a friend and the generation of good hormones include: Reframing a mistake into a learning lesson and it is not "your fault", your friend would ask what the learning experience was. Give any situation your best effort and if it does not work out you are not a "failure", your friend would point out the way you demonstrated your best effort. If you talk to yourself as you would a friend, it increases self acceptance, which is a more positive emotion and leads to a enhanced sense of wellbeing.

WRITE DOWN EVERY DAY EXAMPLES OF HOW I ONLY TALKED TO MYSELF AS I WOULD TO A FRIEND

NOTES

APRIL

1.
2.
3.
4.
5.
6.
7.
8.
9.
10.
11.
12.
13.
14.
15.
16.
17.
18.
19.
20.
21.
22.
23.
24.
25.
26.
27.
28.
29.
30.

NOTES

PILLAR MONTH FIVE

Every time you start to compare stop. The grass always seems greener on the other side of the fence but you ony have a very small "snapshot" of the other person's life. Comparing is an invitation to feeling insecure and more worthless which can only deepen the depression.

People with a healthy sense of self esteem experience feelings of wellness in their bodies that are attributed to the good hormones circulating in their brains for an overall sense of wellbeing. When a person has low self esteem they are even more vulnerable to depression as the stress hormones such as cortisol are present from not feeling safe and secure with themselves and in themselves contributing to depressed brain activity and the depression becomes worse. The insecurity deepens when you compare yourself to others and social media is a breeding ground for viewing everyone who has everything better and more than you do. Social media has been disastrous for the mental wellbeing of teenagers and contributed to an escalation of suicide and depression rates as they compare themselves to their peers and feel less and less valuable in comparison. Social media is only a snapshot of a person's life and of course does not tell the whole story because if it did rich and famous people would never commit suicide such as Kate Spade and Anthony Bourdane The last activity a depressed person needs to do is to start comparing themselves in any way shape or form to anyone else as it will cause the brain to generate the not so good feeling hormones leading to a state of feeling even more depressed. There will always be someone that is richer, smarter, thinner, more famous, the list goes on and on. Plus your focus of attention is on someone else when you need to be circling the attention back around to an activity and focus closer to yourself.

Choose one activity no matter what it is…drawing, baking, organizing files, waxing a car…anything that requires your complete attention and focus for a period of time and that you do not mind doing even better if you really enjoy and even love doing it. Give this activity your complete and undivided attention with the goal that you want to complete it and get a grade of "A" when it is done. If you have this mindset you will have increased concentration and focus so that you become unaware of everything else and get into "the zone" where the focus of attention is on this project and it is all that matters. When you are in This thinking is important because again, you are creating new and different thought patterns in your brain which will help to generate the good hormones and an increased sense of wellbeing. The focus of attention is on what you are doing and what you can do well rather than on someone else and what they have that you do not have. This change in perspective changes everything along with the accompanying activity. You will also have a sense of accomplishment when you are finished with the activity no matter how big or small it does not matter.

The activity does not have to take any more than the time you would take cruising Facebook and social media plus some television time and your brain will have increased good hormones and activity helping to lessen the depression on step at a time.

WRITE DOWN EVERY DAY HOW I DID NOT COMPARE BUT DID AN ACTIVITY THAT INVOLVED MY TOTAL FOCUS

NOTES

MAY

1.
2.
3.
4.
5.
6.
7.
8.
9.
10.
11.
12.
13.
14.
15.
16.
17.
18.
19.
20.
21.
22.
23.
24.
25.
26.
27.
28.
29.
30.
31.

NOTES

PILLAR MONTH SIX

True contentment comes from the inside out. If I am at peace with myself then it will have a positive ripple affect on my entire being this includes recognizing how I am talking to myself and refusing any negativity from outside sources.

Depression carries with it very heavy emotions and a feeling of darkness and heaviness. Any one who has lived it can tell you it is as if you are walking around with one thousand pounds of weights in your head. The heaviness comes from the internal dialogue that will not stop for some people, for others it is feelings of worthlessness and not measuring up, still others have had traumatic experiences. These experiences are all minuses in the brain and the brain knows it by functioning less, producing the stress hormones and the neuron pathways being less active. The brain chemistry is changed by the experiences of the person and how the person interprets those experiences. We know that no two people interpret the same experience the exact same way. I could always feel the heaviness of my brain when my thoughts were negative. Negativity includes thinking about the past, the future, the worst case scenario, rumination (over and over thinking), anger, sadness, fearfulness, aggression, feeling insecure, loneliness, insecurity. This is a big list and there are more so identify the top ones that keep occurring for you and counteract the emotion into one that is the opposite positive emotion. For example, if you are feeling angry think of a situation or person that always makes you feel calm. If you are feeling alone pick up the phone and call someone to say hello. Identifying the negative emotion is crucial as it is generating the stress hormone. Once you start to get in the habit of identifying negativity the time spent on negative emotions can be shortened as you focus on a positive one instead.

Researchers are excited about the growing fields of data that show we can change our depression with brain training, strengthening the brain cells that we already have, which determines the type of experiences that we have. We can sculpt the ability to lessen out depression by recognizing and countering our negative interpretations, replacing them with more positive interpretations and the stress hormones start to fade and be replaced with the hormones that create a feeling of wellbeing. Increased brains cells and activity also take place therefore the depression starts to lesson. The increase in brain activity makes our brain feel lighter because it is working more efficiently and at a greater capacity and our entire outlook becomes brighter.

WRITE DOWN EVERY DAY HOW I STOP ANY NEGATIVE TALK TO MYSELF AND TURN IT TO POSITIVE TALK

NOTES

JUNE

1.
2.
3.
4.
5.
6.
7.
8.
9.
10.
11.
12.
13.
14.
15.
16.
17.
18.
19.
20.
21.
22.
23.
24.
25.
26.
27.
28.
29.
30.

NOTES

PILLAR MONTH SEVEN

Stay in the present moment do not think about the past or the future. Think about today and only the present moment.

It is very easy to get swallowed up in the vicious circle of regrets coming from thoughts of thinking of the past with thoughts such as I wish I would have, could have, should have, and worrying about the future. Of course, all of this is pointless because none of us can change the past and neither can we can we predict the future. All we really have is today and the present moment. When we get stuck in this worry mode our brain is engaging in negative brain activity, producing heavy thinking and of course producing the stress hormones. I think of it like a hamster on a hamster wheel that cannot get off but just keeps running and running and running. This repeated worrying creates a pathway in our brain that becomes easier and easier to fall back into and we fall back into the heaviness of depression. This is a default mode of the brain through our thought patterns which is based on fear and this intensifies our heavy thoughts of depression.

The brain defaults to this mode as it is the survival mode, and it creates this pathway which follows this same track over and over creating the depression. Therefore, pleasant experiences are blocked and we cannot feel the present moment. If we wish to feel more calm and peaceful, we need to engage the part of the brain that is not involved in survival and worrying about the past and future rather focusing on the present moment. This involves rewiring your brain by redirecting your thoughts to the present moment. One way to keep in the present moment is to distract yourself with a change in scenery or activity.

Every time that you catch yourself starting to think about the past or the future catch yourself and tell yourself that all that matters is today and the present moment. When you are relieved of thinking about the mistakes of the past (which you cannot change anyway) and are no longer worrying about the future (which is you have no control over), the heaviness of the thinking lessens. Tell yourself "NOW" or "PRESENT MOMENT" every time you start thinking about the past or the future and redirect your thoughts to something or someone else. Any type of distraction is good so long as it does not involve past or future thinking. Notice how your thoughts of the past and future are heavy and those of the present moment are not full of worry thus not as heavy. Talk to yourself lovingly and patiently. Throughout the day every time you start to worry about the past or future bring yourself back to the present moment as this is how you are rewiring your brain to lessen your depression.

WRITE DOWN EVERY DAY STAYING IN THE PRESENT MOMENT EVERYTIME YOU STARTED WORRYING ABOUT THE PAST AND/OR THE FUTURE.

NOTES

JULY

1.
2.
3.
4.
5.
6.
7.
8.
9.
10.
11.
12.
13.
14.
15.
16.
17.
18.
19.
20.
21.
22.
23.
24.
25.
26.
27.
28.
29.
30.
31.

NOTES

PILLAR MONTH EIGHT

Do something in an entirely different way or do something entirely new.

When you do something in an entirely different way you use different pathways in your brain and begin building neurons or as scientists call it you are increasing your brain neuroplasticity. The same neuroplasticity occurs when you try something entirely new because it is not automatic of course and you have to concentrate and think about what you are doing in a fresh way. When the neuroplasticity is being built the neurons generating are producing the good hormones such as serotonin and oxytocin therefore an increased feeling of wellbeing is felt. Of course while all these wonderful events are happening the stress hormones are decreasing and the accompanying depression is lessening little by little. Every time that you do something different you are activating a different area of your brain and contributing to the feeling of wellbeing and of course overall contentment. That is the difference between the stress hormones in your brain such as cortisol with the state of depression and the good hormones such as oxytocin with the state of wellbeing.

When you are doing something in a different way you need to pay more attention and focus more since it is not so automatic as your brain is firing off more electrical impulses which is good…more activity… the opposite of being depressed! Try brushing your teeth with the opposite hand that you usually brush your teeth with it takes concentration. Try driving to work a different way. If you walk or take the bus try an different way that you have never taken before or a different route. If you are right handed you normally clean with your right hand f course so try cleaning with your left hand for a while, it is really quite a challenge, so you must pay attention. Try skipping backwards…not easy…you have to really pay attention. Try writing with the nondominant hand it is a real challenge. Try doing something new and different that you have never done before just for the heck of it. Other activities that engage the mind that are good choices for neuroplasticity enhancement are crossword puzzles or board games. I have a hard time laughing so listening to a comedy club comedian is a sure way for me to get stretch the data pathways of my serious mind because it outside of the "usual" pattern of thinking for me. Anything that is not automatic and comes easily and naturally to you should be ruled out as you are literally thinking OUTSIDE

THE SAME PATHWAYS TO CREATE NEW ONES OR NEURPLASTICITY. Try something that you have never done before such as enrolling in a class and with so many classes and much online you can literally listen to many topics until you find one that interests you before signing up. If you are up for trying something new make sure that you pick something that you are going to complete so it enjoy it, finish it and it gives you a sense of accomplishment.

WRITE DOWN EVERY DAY WHAT YOU DID IN AN ENTIRELY DIFFERENT WAY(SWITCH WHEN IT BECOMES AUTOMATIC) OR TRY SOMETHING ENTIRELY NEW

NOTES

AUGUST

1.
2.
3.
4.
5.
6.
7.
8.
9.
10.
11.
12.
13.
14.
15.
16.
17.
18.
19.
20.
21.
22.
23.
24.
25.
26.
27.
28.
29.
30.
31.

NOTES

PILLAR MONTH NINE

REMIND YOURSELF THAT YOU HAVE CONTROL OVER VERY LITTLE ...NOT HOW OTHER PEOPLE REACT...THAT OTHER PEOPLE AND EVENTS ARE TRULY OUT OF OUR CONTROL...SEPARATE OTHER PEOPLE AND EVENTS FROM YOUR THOUGHTS ABOUT THEM FROM YOURSELF

The more that we spend time on blaming ourselves for what we "could have done" or "could have said" the further depressed we become and this does not help us. The truth is what is done is done and so much of the outcome simply comes down to TIMING IS EVERYTHING and really has nothing to do with us at all. Of course you need to make sure that you did your very best, but far too often we beat ourselves up and for too long when we need to say "stop it is over and done with I need to move on to something else". STOP TRYING SO HARD!!!!

The depressed person has decreased brain activity

and stress hormones that come with the it which induces further feelings of extreme inferiority about themselves. This in turn creates feelings of worthlessness, self blame, and feeling inferior in every way possible. This depressed mental state is in contrast to a person who has healthy brain activity with the good hormones which then generates the feeling of wellbeing thus they are not they are not susceptible to this type of self induced negativity which then even further drives the depression. That is why depressed people tend to have extreme interpretations while a person in a state of wellbeing does not take everything so personally. You need to remind yourself that you do NOT have control over what most other people say, think and do. If you tend to take on too much responsibility for other people with what is happening or what is not happening, if they are getting along or not, whatever, it is not your duty or job…they are going to do what they are going to do…step back…it is not because of you or not because of you and certainly it is not your fault. You did not say or do the right thing…okay…so what else is new? YOU HAVE CONTROL OVER VERY LITTLE PERIOD!

The depressed person tends to have the negative thoughts go around and around in the same brain pathway and this needs to be changed to a new pathway for neuroplasticity in the brain to occur. Eliminate the black and white all or nothing thinking which this and that you have control over very little. Separate the situation (it is neutral) and say to yourself "This is my thought about this situation and I am separate from the situation and the outcome is not my responsibility". When I started to tell myself that my daughters did not especially want to hang out with each other and there was nothing that I could do about it I was much better off because I removed myself from the situation and it lessened my depression.

The more that you can tell yourself that you have CONTROL OVER VERY LITTLE the less stress you will feel in you mind and body because you realize that YOU ARE SEPARATE FROM THE SITUATION AND/OR PEOPLE THEY ARE NOT YOU AND YOU ARE NOT THEM. This is especially important because remaining more detached and neutral minimizes the tendency to focus on everything that is wrong and the false belief of the control that we have over the situation and/or people as we are taking it less personally. This psychological "distancing" helps to neutralize our emotions which is what is needed in order to keep the stress hormones from being produced and then start to focus on "Hey I am okay no matter what". The brain will start new patterns of thinking with nreuroplasticity and good hormones resulting from changed patterns of thought processes.

WRITE DOWN EVERY DAY HOW YOU REMOVED YOURSELF FROM THE SITUATION OR PERSON(S) WITH A DIFFICULTY (AS YOU HAVE CONTROL OVER VERY LITTLE) AND HOW YOU REMAINED

NEUTRAL BY NOT TAKING IT PERSONALLY OR BLAMING YOURSELF

Take a piece of paper and write down every day what you do correctly, what you have accomplished that day, what has gone well.

SEPTEMBER

1.
2.
3.
4.
5.
6.
7.
8.
9.
10.
11.
12.
13.
14.
15.
16.
17.
18.
19.
20.
21.
22.
23.
24.
25.
26.
27.
28.
29.
30.

NOTES

PILLAR MONTH TEN

REMIND YOURSELF THAT THE LOVE WHICH YOU SEEK IS WITHIN YOU NOW AND YOUR HEART IS BRIMMING WITH IT. PERFORM OR SAY AN ACT THAT CONVEYS LOVE TO ONE PERSON A DAY.

The depressed person feels isolated and alone. When a person is lonely it is difficult to cope and this is a vicious cycle. LONELINESS IS NOT OUR NATURE. HUMAN BEINGS HAVE A NEED TO BELONG. Human beings are social in nature and the depressed person has love and joy in their heart that is just as beautiful as any other person... now is the time to experience this...realize that it has always been there even if you do not believe this it is true! The part of the brain that is functioning in the depressed person and the stress hormones is primarily concerned with survival and the same neural pathways are used over and over (depressed activity). When we behave in a state aligned with love our DNA can be reprogrammed (with higher states of frequencies from these positive emotions) and this can contribute to neuroplasticity (increased neuron activity).

You are reprogramming your thoughts which affect your feelings and emotions for your highest good and you will start to feel little by little that your quality of life is improving. Any gesture big or small COUNTS. COVID-19 has mandated isolation and the result is increased depression among all age groups including elementary school age students. They are isolated from their peers with online schooling, with many obstacles and lack of success that is not addressed with online schooling as it would be in the classroom and ability to connect with peers, teachers and counselors as there is with attendance and participation while physically attending a school. COVID-19 is affecting children of all ages with an increase in sadness and crying at night reported by parents. When people are lonely it is really hard to cope and we are witnessing it with all age groups. The more a person can feel connected and talk to someone the less internalizing and depressed they are likely to feel.

There is convincing evidence from neuroscience researchers regarding how having social interactions and relationships modulate neuroendocrine responses affecting the circulatory system (as well as our brain). Studies have shown that people who are isolated, alone and depressed have an increased risk for stroke and cardiovascular disease. The more you can socialize the less isolated you feel…this goes for committing a daily act that CONVEYS love will connect you more to others and you to them. IT IS NEVER TOO LATE TO FEEL BETTER

ABOUT YOURSELF AND HEAL YOURSELF FROM THE INSIDE OUT...BABY STEPS... ONE STEP AT A TIME AND ONE DAY AT A TIME! Remind yourself every morning that "I have love inside me now and I accept that love to and for myself but I am also going to commit acts and gestures to others as I have this love in me to share". Believe this with your whole heart and soul. Say it as if you mean and believe it and you will find that with consistency and done daily you will feel a little less darkness and a little more light and that is the goal!

WRITE DOWN EVERY DAY EXAMPLES OF CONVEYING LOVE TO ANOTHER PERSON BY A BEHAVIOR OR WORD AND ALSO SAY TO YOURSELF THAT I AM LOVABLE AND HAVE THE LOVE TO SHARE.

NOTES

OCTOBER

1.
2.
3.
4.
5.
6.
7.
8.
9.
10.
11.
12.
13.
14.
15.
16.
17.
18.
19.
20.
21.
22.
23.
24.
25.
26.
27.
28.
29.
30.
31.

NOTES

PILLAR MONTH ELEVEN

EVERY EXPERIENCE THAT I HAVE WITH OTHERS IS A TEACHING EXPERIENCE, ESPECIALLY THE NASTY EXPERIENCES. ASK YOURSELF WHAT CAN I LEARN FROM THIS EXPERIENCE?

Did you ever notice that misery loves company? When someone is feeling miserable they often want to share it with others. This is not an option for the depressed person as you are already feeling low and in a vulnerable state of mind. Every interaction that you have with others has a certain tone or feeling according to the emotions involved and carries with it an energetic frequency. Peace, joy, love, reason, acceptance, neutrality all have higher frequencies than fear, grief, anger so the more neutral you can remain in a nasty experience and try to observe it from "What can this teach me?" also "I will not allow myself to have my emotions involved in these lower frequencies no matter what the other person says." If you can remain as an observer in a sticky situation that has negative emotions you are preserving a higher state of consciousness and the brain will not produce the stress hormones and default to the flat neuron activity in the depressed neural pathways. ASK YOURSELF WHAT CAN I LEARN FROM THIS? If you remain as an observer your thoughts remain more neutral therefore the stress hormones are not generated because you do not get so caught up in the other person's drama. It is important to remind yourself that negative thoughts will carry low energetic frequencies and that you cannot afford to have your thoughts go any lower so DETACHMENT is necessary and NOT ENGAGING is important in order to keep your conscious from lowering in vibration. The depressed person often has guilt, shame and feelings of inadequacy which are all the lowest energetic frequencies so taking on any additional negativity from others is only going to contribute to more depression. The depressed person is also more likely to be too hard on themselves as they are already in this low energetic frequency state. If you tell yourself "THERE IS NO SUCH THING AS A MISTAKE LIFE IS ABOUT LEARNING" then you remove the tendency to be too harsh and critical on yourself. All interactions that we have with others has the possibility of teaching us something and we do not need to get immersed in anything if we remind ourselves that we can be an observer and learner. This DOES NOT mean that you are insignificant quite the contrary. You are monitoring your thoughts and preserving your frequency level which is BENEFITTING

YOUR SENSE OF SELF…very important for the depressed person who often loses their sense of self and being of any value. When you are too critical on yourself it is usually generated from BLACK AND WHITE thinking or ALL OR NOTHING mentality. Remind yourself throughout the day that life is a classroom and I am here to learn without allowing any other situation or person bring me down into lower frequencies. By focusing our attention away from negative things and onto positive things, we can reduce negative emotions and the hormones produced that go along with stress. One way to do this is with cognitive reappraisal. Cognitive reappraisal is the attempt to reinterpret a situation in a way that alters its meaning and changes its emotional impact. When we use cognitive reappraisal, we reframe our situation, this time paying more attention to the good things (or downplaying the bad) again reminding yourself that life is a classroom and I am learning while remaining an observer. When we are struggling with stress, especially stress that we have no control over, cognitive reappraisal can be a really helpful tool and prevent us from lowering our vibration.

EVERY DAY WRITE DOWN AN EXPERIENCE THAT YOU HAD WITH OTHER PEOPLE AND WHAT YOU LEARNED FROM IT. IF IT WAS A NEGATIVE EXPERIENCE WRITE DOWN HOW YOU WERE ABLE TO REMAIN AS AN OBSERVER AND NOT LOWER YOUR ENERGY FREQUENCY.

NOTES

NOVEMBER

1.
2.
3.
4.
5.
6.
7.
8.
9.
10.
11.
12.
13.
14.
15.
16.
17.
18.
19.
20.
21.
22.
23.
24.
25.
26.
27.
28.
29.
30.

NOTES

PILLAR MONTH TWELVE

I WILL GIVE MYSELF A DAILY ACT OF KINDNESS (AS IF GIVING TO A FRIEND) AND BE FULLY PRESENT WHEN I PERFORM THIS ACT.

When a person is in a depression you have difficulty thinking and behaving in a kind way to yourself. Why is it that we can show loving kindness to a pet but we have such a hard time showing the same behavior to ourselves? WE DID NOT ENTER THIS WORLD HATING OURSELVES, but the depression removes any incentive because your thoughts are of a lower vibration. Your emotional state and your self-esteem suffer even more. Our own behavior toward ourselves is negative when we are depressed and not the behavior we would choose for a beloved friend. To counter this lower vibrational state consciously perform an act of kindness to yourself because it carries with it a higher vibration mentally and physically. If you need to psychologically say to yourself "This act of kindness to myself is necessary for increasing my vibration and the positive hormones that come with this will contribute to my brain activity increasing the neurons and pathways. You habitually do not take care or care about yourself when depressed and self-care can plummet. This can be unlearned when you perform one act a day of kindness or self-care whether you feel like it or not. SHOW YOURSELF LOVE WITH A DAILY BEHAVIOR OF CARING FOR YOURSELF. Depression directs us to ignore our self-care so when we do an act of caring for our physical body the emotional the feeling of being "worth it" increases a little bit at a time.

When you are tempted to behave in a way that is not respectful and caring toward yourself you subconsciously are telling yourself "I do not matter" so ask yourself "would I do this to my friend or pet?' The smallest and most routine of behaviors can matter if you really pay attention to what you are doing and you are staying in the present moment. Focus only on single tasks. Do the task slowly, at a relaxed pace and pay attention the whole time no matter how small the task is, take it in and enjoy it. Tell yourself "Now I am brushing my teeth more thoroughly than I ever have". As you do something simply tell yourself what you are doing and do only that task. Some examples of small but caring behavior could be putting lotion on your chapped lips or hands. Eating slowly and thoroughly after choosing something healthy to eat. Eating a favorite snack as a treat after a long day.

DECEMBER

1.
2.
3.
4.
5.
6.
7.
8.
9.
10.
11.
12.
13.
14.
15.
16.
17.
18.
19.
20.
21.
22.
23.
24.
25.
26.
27.
28.
29.
30.
31.

www.ingramcontent.com/pod-product-compliance
Lightning Source LLC
Chambersburg PA
CBHW041131110526
44592CB00020B/2764